# Repurposed

# Repurposed

## Trial by Lineation

Poems

by Anthony Andricks

www.AnthonyAndricks.com

979-8-9898989-0-9 (Paperback)
979-8-9898989-1-6 (Hardcover)
979-8-9898989-2-3 (Digital)
979-8-9898989-3-0 (Color Paperback)
979-8-9898989-4-7 (Audiobook)

Library of Congress Control Number: *Forthcoming*

Book design by Glen Edelstein, Hudson Valley Book Design

*For Geraldine (Gerry) Sheridan and Ryan Findley,*
*each without whom this book would not exist*
*(and perhaps neither would I).*

# Contents

## III. Those That Are Me

The world needs your light.

# Author's Note

True, deep, and honest human-to-human connection is the most important thing that we will experience during our lifetimes. We don't have long on this earth, and experiences unshared disappear meaninglessly into the void. If we hide who and what we are, there can be no shared experience.

I seek to share with *you*, Dear Reader.

The words that follow are about pain, suffering, healing, solace, rising above, and repurposing of self.

For we may be damaged, but it is possible—without leaving behind all that shaped us and all that we were—to become something new, something warm, something content, something beautiful, and something useful—in ways unimagined.

*Love,*
*-A*

# I. Those Before Me

# Atascadero

What did you do, Ocho,
    To be trapped with me inside these concrete walls?
    To swelter here?
    To count the beads of sweat that sting my eyes?

Did your legs wander, Ocho?
Did they wrap around tu amigo, like mine?
Do they vibrate love codes through the wall
To your secret lover on the other side?

I'm doing well. Thanks for asking, Ocho.
You can call me Gene. I'm sixteen.
Please stay up there in the corner.
I'd hate to squash you in my sleep.

This is Matt, Ocho, where I lie down.
Yeah, I know he's skinny, Ocho.
He's only slightly fatter than the ground.

Do you smell the burning, Ocho, of
Those buzzing loud machines?
The frying minds of our brothers?
Do you hear their useless pleas?

Give me jazz hands, Ocho,
to swat away the Anectine.
Don't let them drown me, Ocho.
I hear them coming now for me.

Ocho, please don't leave!
Raise that top hat.
Twirl that cane.
When you're dancing, Ocho,
I can barely feel the pain.

Bravo, Ocho!

Bravo!

Brav—

# 1849 Journal #1

The water is magic in these parts, says Elu
Not the marshes, slick with mud and thick with mosquitos,
but the water trapped just beneath
the rock and clay

The natives say
the aquifers hold
the Memegwesi at bay

For those mischievous water spirits
would surely pour out confusion
upon the white men
who have invaded and stolen these lands.

# Shine

Two generations back
lived a girl born out of time
Her cheeks betrayed the Cherokee
two more generations yet behind
And she'd outwit all the boys
what kept her in line
A valedictorian and a beauty
By them muted and defined
And she'd play along because
those were the times

She loved her lord
and her living showed it
Her god's love in the flesh to make them know it
To love as her lord loved her
(As she understood it)
Never leaving, never forsaking

And when that chaw chewin' preacher
Flit the demarcation line
She'd bear him daughters, never sons,
And his plate at suppertime
She'd be a good soldier's girl
and when she died
They'd praise her—wife and mother
But those were not her
Shine:

Keeping sheathed
Nanye'hi's bow
Never waving the swan's wing
In an undeserving world
Controlled
by adolescent kings.

# Monsters

Movements and monsters
Breeding Victorian royal families
Birthing shades of abnormal
And basement mutations

> They sent their sons into
> The dark streets
> Stealing away all light
> Crying abomination
> When refuge be found in
> Leather, sweat, and smoke

They cried *punishment*
When the blood turned

Let them die alone

> Be buried

> Alone.

Monsters and movements
Rising and falling empires
Breeding fighters and haters
And pious hypocrites

Faith birthing abandonment
birthing debauchery
birthing self-fulfilled prophecy
birthing rebellion
birthing abandonment

Monsters creating movements
        Creating monsters

# Gentlemen's Jig

Tap dance
Game of chance
Fuck romance
Stick it under

Swipe of hand
Be a man
Knees on land
Stick it under

Bend down
Look around
He's a hound
Stick it under

Stand tall
Face the wall
Fingers call
Stick it through

Make it hard
Punch the card
Thank your guard
Abandon crew

# 1849 Journal #2

They say the Memegwesi will steal into your home at night
and make off with your bread or boots
or exchange your sugar with your salt

But the Mshignebig
swallows whole the largest of men
and the Mshibzhii
drags them under
to a deep
drowning death

# Fast Friends

I wish I could have known them

then.

Cigarettes hanging from their lips
Hippy hair (his and hers)
Bell bottoms and short shorts
Rheingold and Coors, and
Devil may care.

I bet I would have liked them

then.

The sneak outs and sneak arounds
At parties in polyester
With Lucy and Mary Jane
Floors covered in corduroy.

I wish I could have known them

then.

Might've been fast friends

before
the radio teachers
and grifters and preachers
came
to steal their hearts
away.

# A Place to Say We Were

You suggest a bar where the
pretzels were staler than
your dad's third marriage.

    I say Jack's basement where you
    broke a PlayStation controller
    in a fit
    of adolescent rage.

Then there was the spilt beer
and how
we said at the same time
not to cry over it,
and we memorized the spread
of the Buckeyes / Wolverines
instant classic.

You said if anyone recognizes you
while we're out, I'm your cousin.

Remember how drunk
we got on my sixteenth?

    Tell that story.

        And one time I had to.

You said
be specific but not too specific
or they'll sound like guilty details,

and I tried my best.

That one night I told you
to slap my ass
as a joke to throw them off,
and I think it worked.

Your head on my shoulder,
we settled on stale pretzels and
Mortal Kombat 3.

We agreed that
memorizing a fatality would be
a guilty detail

before

heading home to our families.

*The settlers scorn the legends of the Odawa*
*while holding tight to their own myths*
*Be they told by native or settler*
*they are all stories to me*
*Lessons that bring an understanding*
*of the storyteller himself*
*his history*
*what he holds dear*
*what he fears*
*what he hopes to become*

# Gloves

I still hear his laugh
when I slip my hands
into these gloves

I hear Crash Bandicoot
buttons smashing
and the lighter firing up a hit

I hear the spokes of the bicycle turning,
Max barking in the basket,
and the Grand Rapids rushing alongside

I hear NFL whistles,
common-sense liberal politicking,
and Auntie boasting of his generosity
(while polishing the evidence)

I see his face blushing
when one of us reveals too much
but never with judgment

I see working hands
and the love in their lines

I hear a chopper whirring
somewhere above a jungle
and the voice of a man that lost so much
give thanks to have us, just as we are

Oh, to have one more good day
for her, for us

One more day
to tell him all the things I know

When I warm my hands
in his gloves.

# Pay It No Mind

Mild-mannered Queen, a Saint of the Streets
A Nobody from Nowheresville, on perpetual parade
Begs for a dollar, then gives it away
To a hungry child, scalded and scarred
Left to surf alleys and piers,
Discarded.

Then pushed.

Strong Black Queen in colorful trash
She-wolf under the blazing moon
Collects bricks for her sack
Brings Christmas in June
Makes sugar plums dance on those
Betty Badge vrooms
Glass walks in heels
on Christopher Street
Stomps and crunches
Her radical feet
Sets inside fires out
*Let the Peggy Piggies burn*
*Let them smell this floral crown*
*Let Lily Law learn*

Then shunned.
Pays the price for living in the sun.

Serves up Hot Peaches
Works hotels by the hour
Can't work nowhere else

When you're a Saint of the Streets.

# 1849 Journal #4

The native legends are tied
to the land itself
connected from the veins
of the body
through the roots
of the trees
and downwards into the plumes
in the depths of the earth
The Natives are an extension
of the earth itself
or perhaps its consciousness
And who are we
to scoff at that?

# Knotting Balloons

On that day,
these chords will be pure

No skipping on the tops of heads
of those submerged
up to the neck

No choking on silverware

No trading autographs
for genuflecting favors
under banquet tables

I know how the earth spins
a little faster since Sendai
when Gaea pulled her arms in
a little tighter to her chest

And the swine are barely masked

The smell of brandy and cigars
and the atlas in the study
opens up into a bar

Clenching tongs, clinking ice
It's all so very NYSE
'Sell' is the advice

So go for par
on the green
of the office limousine
and never let her
make you ask her twice

# Grotesque

Dr. H. Anonymous
wore a hideous mask

freshly plucked
from the corpse
of a movie killer
served his final blow

and made of human skin—
the skin of its victims
bladed by scholarship

Those whitecoats
call us sick

imprison us and torture us
        until
we fulfill their theories
and predictions
and classifications
and

then they boast

But Dr. H proclaims:

I wear a white coat
          too,
               you see
Look into these eyes—
these black, cavernous eyes

Look into this mask
          and
see your reflection

# Silver Hill Sally

A moat of milk and honey flows
    around Silver Hill
so sweetly stinging the senses

And

In the new promised land
    No daughters of Ham
Shall be shown mercy

For God has seen the detestable things among them

Let this one take the lightning of God
into her temples
For she is not in His

Let this idolator of knowledge
know His might
That she may be reborn

and take a man

# 1849 Journal #5

We have invaded these lands
with arms and disease
We have driven them into islands
and made them prisoners

I dare not speak such words out loud
lest they close their purses to me,
or worse, drive me from the town

# Incubi

Right middle finger
pulls the glove down the
center of the left arm
to the elbow

Fingers taught and spread
and covered in white satin

Proper.

Classy.

Elegant.

Sophisticated.

Elbow pads
and talk of investments,
monogramed money clips,
box seats,
taxes,
and mistresses

A beauty spot
Hands that glide slowly
down the sides of the breasts
and the hips

Fabric clinging
to ample curves

And talk of investments,
monogramed money clips,
box seats, and
taxes

And whispers of
absent wives

# Incision

I see something in you
That's inside of me
I'll cut it out of you
To cut it out of me

# 2020 Westwood

Most men…

Thwomped
    (but they glided)
Stammered
    (they orated)
Clowned
    (they entertained)
Wore
    (they dressed)
Bobbed
    (they danced)
Combed
    (they styled)

I was not like them,
and I was

"Meet yourself"
They said, and
they were somewhat right

I liked the way they styled my comb
But not the way they dressed my wore

I liked the way they danced my bob
For Saturday nights on the dance floor

But mostly I loved them for existing
And inspiring me to be

Together, to

Believe.

# II. Those That Were Me

# Bleach

If I drink this bleach,
Will I stop sinning?
Will I go to heaven?

I may drink this bleach
after Pipe Land Level 7.

# 1849 Journal #6

*Everything moves like water*
*flowing inseparably*
*relentlessly changing*
*shape and form*

*Water brings life and sustains it*
*and owing to these things*
 *is not water as much*
*a god*
*as any?*

# Calling the Elements

He tried fervently to conjure a god to love him
  with backyard dirt,
    desk fan wind,
      drugstore candles,
        and bathtub water.

*Tomorrow,*
*Elu has promised*
*to teach me the ways of water magic*

*and I will hold my mind and heart*
*open to receive*

# The Girl Next Door

We love Chicago,
Waffle cones dripping
With cherry-chocolate chunks,
Wooly soft ones,
Shrews, mongooses, and the like

And words like *sundries*

One look
Writes me a novel,

Gives complex assembly instructions,

Or brings me to hysterics

And, although here
It's dangerous to go alone...

I'm fairly certain that
On some version of earth in the multiverse,

We fuck.

[Epilogue: She'd be insulted if we didn't]

# Safe

In his teenage bedroom
somewhat safe
from the world

Letting
those sweet layered
mezzo soprano
flames
engulf him

With unique enunciation
and inflection

In a language, he thought,
only he could understand:

You are not alone.

And in those moments,
he believed
and was believed—

When the door
was closed.

# Gay A's

How many A's do I need
    To be as good as their B's?

# Unbelievable
## / unbelievable

Watch me ace this stoichiometry exam
And take the silver medal on the National Latin Exam
Watch me ruin the curve
Where derivatives are concerned
And sit first chair in symphonic band

      I'll be Unbelievable.

        and

      If I were a queen, I'd win the
      Whole fuckin' Drag Race, honey
      and if I were Heere, I'd make
      all the goddamn money

I'd be Unbelievable.

      Look at me achieve, mommy.
      Look at me succeed, daddy.
      I'm still good (even in these heels), and
      I'm still good (even with this lazy wrist)

        so

Feel this fire that they started
Burn for decades
All because they found me

        unbelievable.

# Blue

So many nights
he cried and cried
He killed her with
a teenage mercy wish

A fleeting moment
a flicker
of a prayer
for the pain to end

And death is
misunderstood
until it reaches out
for a heart close to yours
and claims it for
the Cosmos

He relearns each night
in the dark
that she's not there
That he'll never
see her face again
Never hear
her laugh again

And it confuses

So simple yet
so incomprehensible
for a mind inchoate

How can there
be a tomorrow?

How can you kiss
Blue lips?

How do you say goodbye
to a piece of you?

And then one day
years later
he suddenly understands:

Blue lips at birth
Blue veins
Blue earth
Blue waves
Blue eyes sometimes
Blue nights
Blue days
Blue lips at the end
Blue
Always.

# High School Boys

In high school
there were two kinds of boys—

Boys who didn't want to
piss at a urinal
too close to
the faggot

and

boys who stood up for
a friend.

Like Stocky Brocky
who would go off-roading
in Astro Vans
and make you think:

*Maybe it wouldn't be so bad*
*To be a Christian,*
*Or at least*
*One of the good ones.*

# And. . .Still

All is Sisyphean
but this rock, it is not mine
sweat disperses
in parallel time
and
although this is expensive wine
still
the sarsen is not mine

All is Odyssean
but Penelope is not mine
this arrow flies
fast in line
and
although the journey is sublime
still
the maiden is not mine

All is Dionysian
but this feast, it is not mine
glasses raised
they finely dine
and
Circe may turn them to swine
still
this banquet is not mine

All is Utopian
But the garden is not mine
fruit hangs low
with tempting shine
and
although the serpent winds behind
still
this garden is not mine

# Clementines

There was a time
when I'd call ahead to the restaurant
and have the table prepared
with fresh fruit
and flowers

When I would lose myself
in your eyes

and lose myself.

When I would love so deeply
you
who loved me before anyone else

before my mother and father
before my god
before me

You held me, and suddenly I was

Unabandoned

Claimed

Then there was goose liver pate
lobster bisque
bald head slaps and
forks in our eyes

And a taste of what it was like to
at last be loved

And then I lost myself.

And then
you were

gone.

# 1849 Journal #8

*Tomorrow I will hang*
*and I expect the townsfolk*
*will cheer with glee*

*They have taken everything from me.*
*My dignity,*
*my freedom,*
*my Love,*
*and tomorrow,*
*my life.*

# Slice

Make them deep enough
to hurt

    until the outside
    matches the backs of

your eyes

# The March of the Beast

He was swallowed by a beast
born the same as Athena
from a pregnant pain inside

Stealing pieces of flesh and sanity
from its captive host

Ingesting and gestating
devouring every chemical
responsible for joy

Until he was bruised
and bedridden
and
settling for his own
saltwater.

        And the beast would sing
        from the inside
        in screeching cacophonies:

        *Why do you starve that African boy?*
        *Why do you torture those homeless strays?*

        *You worthless shit.*
        *Feed me,*
        *You worthless shit!*

His hands, no longer his own
They could not brew
or serve
or sustain

For the beast preferred
its tendons rare
and atrophied.

Sing, my beast! My Oedipus, sing!

And when it was birthed,
he looked upon it
and wept.

Guilty for what he had made—
what it had brought him to be.

So, he would compose a March
of single strain and snare:

*The Lure of the Apostle*

To lead them down the hatch—
those little green serpents
one by one, then two by two

slithering inward and downward
to keep the beast at bay.

To finally fade away.

# Where were you when...?

Hair isn't deserved, so he shaves it to the skin
Clothes represent, so he wears a costume to fit in

Food is a comfort, so he searches dark places for coins
to buy a cup of noodles—the first in two days
and for dessert, a half-smoked cigarette
from a public ashtray

Others steal and blame him
Why wouldn't they?
He's such a likely suspect
They don't owe him anything

Too weak to work and sometimes to move
Only strong enough to sleep
in a borrowed living room

He sleeps for days and dreams of war, then
Boom!

He awakens to a fuzzy screen at precisely 9:03
A plane explodes into a building on a staticky tv

In the fog of hunger

this could still be a dream
But his greatest wish just then
is for buttered toast
and coffee
with sugar
and cream

# 1849 Journal #9

*I am broken*
*Surely death will not be*
*as painful as this life*

*I only hope that THE Creator*
*is not their creator*
*Who hates*
*and judges*
*and breaks the hearts*
*and spirits of men—*

*who would bring fire and damnation*
*upon all who do not succumb*
*to their murderous tendencies*
*cloaked in the sweet*
*melodies of worship*

# Antichrist

I dreamt
I was the antichrist
and you were
Doris Day

The four dark steeds,
in fiery haze,
are on their
merry way

Dancing on
the northern winds
How long will they stay?

They'll gallop here
for seven years
to maim, kill, and fillet

This sinner's soul
on cruise control
Route six hundred sixty-six
Beyond salvation
hanging on
a precious crucifix

The one I sang to as a child
the king of all the land
Psychotic fear,
the kingdom near
will fall by my own hand

I dream I am the antichrist
and you are Doris Day
This is what I see
when darkness veils the eyes

Subconsciously
still swimming here
in programmed childhood lies

# 1849 Journal #10

*It has been more than*
*fifty and one hundred years*
*since witches burned in Salem*

*yet the evil hearts of those accusers*
*have found their way westward*
*to the Great Black Swamp of Ohio*

*and have found, in me,*
*a new witch*
*to abhor*

# 1849 Journal #11

It is not enough for them
that I should die
That they will break my neck
and bulge my eyes

No.
They demand audience to my demise

For only earlier this evening
they tore asunder
the blockades erected
by my executioners
to shield my death from public eye

They would not have it

They seek to hear my bones cracking
and revel in my limbs flailing

to raise their arms upward
to sway in synchronization
with my lifeless corpse

# 1849 Journal #12

I know that many
believe I am guilty

and were I guilty,
would I not deserve
what tomorrow brings?

But there is no empathy
left in me

They have seen to that, no doubt

I hate them all.

And wherever my Creator
takes me at sunset,
oh, may I find Elu
waiting there for me

I long to see his face again,
to hear his laugh,
to feel his hands
in mine

# Mistakes

A vice grip on the rose rim
At the morning sun

A forced implosion looming
A backfired silver gun

A majestic twelve-foot wingspan
In a shanty six by eight

A predestined cherry smiling
Atop a bowl of fate

How hard he swings his hammer
But the wall, it never breaks

Humans, we are follies
Nature's best mistakes

We once enslaved each other
And now we forge a cage

To bind our own contentment
And fill ourselves with rage

So, he builds himself a curtain
Down the center of his mind
That cannot be drawn open
Forged of the iron kind

Yearn for the impossible,
No matter what it takes!
This is the everlasting plight
Of nature's best mistakes

# Potato Salad

I was born and raised inside a bland potato salad / and jiggly desserts with raisins and Jell-O. / It's a miracle my sister is a pastry chef / and I can't even *make* a potato salad. / My brain won't let me try. / All my adult life has been spent / in search of spices / that didn't grow in the county seat— / that red sea / that can't see over those candy-Jericho walls / or under the water of those artesian wells. / But I've known some good miners and snorkelers there / and everywhere. / How will I Iearn to make the perfect potato salad? / First, I must understand the recipe, its roots, and all its flavors. / Tell me about your grandmother who brought it to July 4th picnics. / Tell me what you tasted then / and I'll add some spices to my rack.

# Two Black Crows

Eye to eye
They stare
Into ocular mirrors
Each as ominous as the other
They flap and flap
Conducting the air into
A fugitive symphony

Each hates himself
But loves the other
In dichotomous refrain

*His feathers are like mine*, each thinks
But cannot break his gaze

Their dance is brave
Back and forth
Obvious, they know

And both are left in limbo, then—
Stalemate.
Two black crows.

# Evasive Knight

The air is strange and lemmings new
I reappear, possessions few
The day is long, the night is warm
And there my song takes subtle form

Where I sleep, this borrowed bed,
Brings flowers to this restless head
And caps me with a cozy crown
That cruel time will soon take down

This rose, it blooms
I bid it not
But Venus churns her magic pot
And years of old begin anew
Damn her poison!
Damn her brew!

My head is loud
My heart more still
Trapped on this Sisyphean hill
What I desire will not be mine
Not in this life
Not in this time

The shot he took meandered west
Eros missed his brawny chest
It lodged within the poplar tree
He flew away
then laughed at me

So here I sit
where all have sat
The one he missed
can tell of that
Wondering how
to move my pawn
With my Knight
already gone.

# 1849 Journal #13

*Oh, Elu, I hope you do not blame me*
*Forgive my blindness*
*to the evils you foretold*

*Please embrace me and hide me*
*under your warm bearskin cloak*

*Reveal to me the secrets of my spirit*
*and where it is going*

*Show mercy upon me,*

*Eluwilussit.*

# III. Those That Are Me

# Burn

This conversation, this night,
I unzipped my soul
(if I believed in souls)
I'll suck it down, black powder,
and let it cover my lungs
in carcinogens

I will let it burn my fingers
into blisters.

I will let this night scar me
to remember
what I never almost had.

It was never mine.

Never
almost
mine.

# A Gemini Ditty

A1: A hot chicken sandwich
    A2: A salad of greens
A1: A few cigarettes
    A2: A nicotine patch
A1: Sex in the woods
    A2: And abstinence
A1: Abandoning regrets
    A2: A chastity latch

A1 and A2:
Warm purring fuzzies
Both snuggled on feet
An old Tori record, it
Spins on repeat

A1:  Now the moon shines
    A2: the sun rays
A1: And the song sings
    A2: the wind stings
A1: I can rest my head
    A2: I am wide awake

A1: Stretch my arms and my feet
    A2: Use my hands and my head
A1: With the air set to heat
    A2: To honor the dead

A1: So, get the fuck out…
            A2: Saying prayers in…

A1 and A2:
My bed.

# Love Lines

Can you draw a line from pain to love
without picking up your pencil?

Can you ever separate the circles of
the Venn Diagram?

Will you let me love the pain away?

Will you love mine away?

# Inherit the Windy

The intricate bird feeder
His hands bled to make
is a sight to behold

BUT IT KILLED A TREE, MURDERER

And that seed
isn't the healthiest

And if birds are fed for free
they won't learn how to forage

So go back to your own country
BIRD KILLER

HE WANTS TO KILL ALL THE BIRDS

Can you imagine no birds?
Empty skies?

First no birds
then no planes
no travel
no cars
no walking
no moving

We'll all be vegetables
rotting in place
because of that feeder
his hands bled to make

# The Sticky Place

A strange paradox
Created by the mind
Confined inside it

A carefully constructed prison
Utilitarian
yet cozy

A scrim
to shield full view of
the leading man
from the cold
stares of the crowd

Give your anger
and
your drunken rambles
to his silhouette.

All you get
is
shadow

# Taproot

Why is the dandelion yellow?
Because god designed it that way.
My condolences to the botanist,
and a fond farewell
to the botanical establishment.

# Shooter

I wanted to vomit
when I heard the shooter
shared my name
Today I hate my name

I lost my eyes
when I heard the shooter
shared my age
Today I hate my age

Today I am a Spartan
But I have also been a Rebel,
An Eagle,
A Raider,
and so many things
and so many children

We have died a thousand times
Pierced
and shredded
And yet we beg:
Kill me again, please.
Kill me again.

Today I hate my name.

# Prayers

Let me loose
like a mumbled word
echoed
under SPACIOUS SKIES

Set me free
from this chamber
with the gentle squeeze
of your finger

To fly o'er
AMBER WAVES OF GRAIN

See them blossom on the ground—
these strangely FRUITED PLAINS

AMERICA, AMERICA
No will
and no mercy

So, holes in heads
Will CROWN THY dead

For one and all
TO SEE

# Spy Balloon

Everything is a thing / For a time / Spotted, picked up, scooped / Bantered on about /

Debated, spun, capitalized upon / Satirized, memed, scrolled / Mythologized

then forgotten / Everything is art / Held within a lens / reflected through

/ A billion unique prescriptions / Framed, judged / Appreciated and

despised / Appraised, bought, and sold / Coveted then worthless

/ Everything is a spy balloon / Harmless then harmful /

Obsessing and possessing / Encompassing and

enthralling / Swiping into frenzy / Until

missiles are launched / Into the sky

/ To bring them down / Every-

thing is a thing / For

a moment / and

then it is

not.

# Mommies

Some people are sad
      those children don't have a father
Unless they have
      a single mother

# Uncertainty Principle

A word vortex
s w i r l s
inside
from ear to ear
orbital electrons and protons
fire at random
and at will

An orgy of syllables and ideas
slithers in and out of one another
moaning and sighing, but
never fully interlocking
never precisely captured
without dilution
of
displacement

# Oopsie

Sometimes words come too quickly—
in premature lineation.

# Red Rain

Infinitely tumbling
along the circumference
of societal sphere

No force to counterbalance

Grasping for flags
whizzing past, loosely planted

    by professors
    and influencers
    and breaking newscasters

Eager marionettes dancing
    desperate for applause
        and validation

Ready to boot others from orbit
    with a swift kick
        as they spin by holding
            last week's flag or
            yesterday's flag or
            last hour's flag

            to vilify and destroy
            and self-aggrandize

until the kicker is kicked,
    and the kicker is kicked,
        and the kicker is kicked

Until they yank
their strings so hard
they slice the ivory hand above

At last, to dance their
own dance
under the
red
rain

# Giddyup!

The horsemen are whispering
Little girls giddy at a sleepover

They taste our disdain
long licking the sweat
rolling down our furrowed brows

Pillows fluffed and piggy tails tied
they smell the rotting stench of us

They giggle out secrets
And write them out in code:

N-E-I-G-H (or N-I-G-H?)

They know

        we toss pink petals
        before the hooves of eager steeds
        We struggle in manmade currents

Brushing tangled and fiery manes
        they writhe against
                those saddles in satisfaction

patiently waiting for us
to come undone

# Moonlight

The moon is in the sky,
    but you aren't looking.

    Well?

    Why aren't you?

# Effeminate Domain

Take ye, Governor,
for this is my body

This, do in remembrance of
my platforms and lashes

Take ye my joy,
my wigs, my nails

For I have no womb
for your brandy glasses

to command

Take ye, Lieutenant,
for this is my ass

Break it, your bread,
my saintly daddy

Take ye my youth,
my locks, my lips

For I have no womb
for your cigar caddy
to encase

Take ye, gentlemen, and
use our bodies

to

transubstantiate

# Lightning

I found him
Under the orange Thailand sun
Beneath the pink full moon
In the graces of a Goddess of Water
Well-pleased by our Krathong

She sent
Lightning in a sea cloud
To decorate the sunset sky
It hovered high above our bobbing vessels
And reflected in his eyes

I found him
On a moonlit beach in Krabi
A glass in one hand
In the other, a bottle of wine

And we talked with the night
Until our toes touched high tide
And steadfast doctrines unraveled
In my mind

I found him
In Phuket, Maya Bay, and Chang Mai

I found him
in the sand, in the water, in the sky

I found him
Soaked in the streets of Bangkok
Singing Songkran with the Thai

I found him
nineteen stories higher
in my arms, behind my eyes

I found him in the sadness of goodbyes

# Those Never Work

Drip, drip, drip
    to dehydrated heart
    aged ten years in a barrel

        He thaws and massages it
        to life
        with a warmness
        Contrived

It will not sustain
        as we peel the magical
            to reveal the mundane

As embraces become thumbs
coding the distance

As lips are pulled
1,332 miles apart

It beats
like honey
        on the tongue
            for the first time

But the spell was broken
somewhere mid-Atlantic

Where the heat of the convenient
sang the Siren's song

Where nearer arms could wrap
around his body
less comfortably
unmagically

and

His AI rewrites the code
To erase the Glow.

But this heart, revived
still pumps fresh blood

and

remembers his predictions of
foreign groomsmen

and

yearns for restoration
            that will never come

# R&R

On nights
when all is still
and silent,
the second hand,
a metronome,
paces songs
the world will never hear.

They die like mayflies.

But a harmony of purrs
regulates another
metronome inside
and slows its
rhythm to a
whole
rest.

# Nature to Nature

Snow covered toothpick trees beyond a crooked wooden fence
White-spotted wings hawking the sun-soaked skies
A midwinter wetland, hidden and preserved
An unpaved paradise unseen and unheard

Save the boys of nature, some who plant their seed
atop the frozen ground and withered weed

The proof is in the bootprints
and where the paths converge

Somewhere behind a thistle where they merge

to melt the winter ice
and blues

To bring nature
to nature.

# Edison

Some days
the sunlight makes
a playground

Some days
the sunlight
illuminates
my imperfections

Some days
the sunlight
calls me close

and

Some days
the sunlight
brightens only
the world outside

But when he switches on,
I don't need the sunlight
I don't need the sun
for anything at all

Give me the rain.

Give me the fall.

I don't need anything else
at all.

# Crustacean

Body is home
This house is haunted
The paint is chipped and worn
And the sounds, oh the sounds
Spiderweb windows
Make six of him as he struggles
To peer through

And there he is inside
The same as before.

Body is shell
With a fresh coat
And a few extra pounds
Up and down
In some of the right places

And there he is inside
The same as before.

# Molasses

The weight of arm
And warmth of breath.

Sandpaper jaws
Scrubbing mine.

Fit so well
Into curve.

Frozen,
Burning "S"
Into sheets.

Couldn't halt the high.

Couldn't dip
Those feet in
Molasses.

# IV. Repurposed

# Joy

The smell of feet
     emanating from
          shoes kicked off
               after work.

The sight of friends
     in London
          you may have never
               seen again.

The sound of kitten's chirp
     at taunting
          window birds.

The touch of the cozy
     waffle blanket
          pulled over
               bare legs.

The taste of dinner
     made by anyone
          other than
               yourself.

# Get Fucked

Generalized Anxiety Disorder,
Go fuck yourself.

Emotional Dysregulation,
Go fuck yourself.

Rejection Sensitive Dysphoria,
Go fuck yourself.

Social Anxiety Disorder,
Go fuck yourself.

Mood stabilizers,
Go fuck yourself.

Still. Fucking. Standing.

# Ukrainian Heart

How do you keep a heart
Alive
under siege?

When bombs are falling
And stones are crumbling

When spirits are fading
And allies are wavering

When enemies
March slowly through
Chambers and ventricles
To wear you down
To stifle circulation
To break
You.

You
Fight.

You drown them
In your blood

You pump them left to right.

For as long as it takes
Until
You have

Reclaimed.

# The Steward of Duck Ledges

No more electronic chimes or perfectly syncopated vibrations
Screaming into my head
with best regards and preemptive gratitude
To abscond from
the time jockeys
and the careful nudging
To save these raw red hands
from wringing
And this back
From rocking

To trade it all
To bark with the sea lion
To dive with the razorbill
To nest with the puffin

No more crafted choreography or publicly pious soldiering
Guilting my conscience with temptation, inadequacy, and doubt
To scuttle from
Worldwide Dorians Gray
And virtuous grandstanding
To save this brain
From sticking
And these eyes
From fading

To trade it all
To sing with the nor'easter
To clap with the waves
To wade with the rocks

And don't you know
Billy understands the value of solitude
and the beauty of nature:

There is no emptiness in it
and doesn't have to be.

# On Stealing Time

Somewhere inside I think I knew—
the night he drove an hour
with flowers
through the phantom zone
    across state lines
        to the gas station
            where I worked
                while failing to piece my life
                back together.

A boombox moment undeserved.

But I forced myself to yes,
to comfortable,
too comfortable,
for too many seasons.

Perhaps I stole those years from Passion, and she left me cold.
    I wouldn't give them back—
        butterfly effect and all.

But,
all these years later,
    I hope he has someone by his side
        who knows how to keep
            his blossoms alive.

# La Isla Isabela

On Isla Isabela
I saw my beginning
In
My long black reptilian tail
My bright orange claws
My smooth gray dorsum
Piercing the crystal waters
Polka-dotted by
The equatorial sun

I saw my beginning
In
My floppy blue feet
My slippery flippers
My fusiform tuxedo
Perched on a lonely rock
Slick with sea slime

I saw my beginning
In
My giant highland shell
My mighty hammer head
My curlicue tail
Anchored fast against
The underwater tow

And

I saw my ending
In
The gummy munch of a
Toothless tortoise
A slender fish skewered by
A bladelike beak
And in the eyes of
A fellow traveler
On life's
Last adventure

# If *You* Couldn't

They create a world unto themselves,
      a language of their own

Songs the masters may not sing and
      words the preachers may not speak

They jazz
They produce
They vogue

And do not strangle with broken chains
      but suffocate with art and beauty
         with talent and style

And do not fight with justified fists
      but punch creation through the Veil

They entertain (but are not for your entertainment)

They are everything you are (but are not for you)

As believable as you (but not believed)

In pain like you (but not relieved)

But more (than you)
And less (than you, you think)

111

For they couldn't have earned it
        if *you* couldn't

So, they'll keep outworking
and out-creating
until

They are gods,
and you are men

        and they are gods of men.

# Boulders

All of us are rolling boulders
of varying mass
and with varying mass
At $y = 0$, with luck
but often slanted
in infinite directions:

Invisible boulders,
Noticeable boulders,
Concealed boulders,
Obvious boulders,

with advantages
and handicaps
and obstacles
and catalysts.

Roll your boulder
if you can,
and when a hand is free
roll another's.

# Midwestern Wizard

No magic powers
No little black bag
No hot air balloon
No emerald swag

No platitudes to ground you
Or wishes for the granting
Just his arms around you
When you feel like landing

And he will be your Kansas
But he'll never be your Oz
This wizard isn't capable
Of breaking natural laws

He will not heal your wounds
Or be your great escape
Just your average wizard
In his homemade bed sheet cape

He will not be the jacket
On the puddle that you're crossing
Or the brick-laid road
That takes you where you're going

But he will be your Kansas
With his steadfast, sturdy plains
To keep you standing firmly
When you are home again

No platitudes to ground you
Or wishes for the granting
Just his arms around you
When you feel like landing

# No Time Like the Present

Why do we always say
      *he lit up the room*
after someone dies?
Is it true, or just something we say?
If someone you know
Lights up the room
Why not tell her so
*Today?*

# On the Bus to Reykjavik

The birds move with a strange cadence
Bjork emanates from two headsets
The mountain curvature is less Vogue
    and more Jessica Rabbit
The fog tiptoes with purpose over
a landscape of cookies and cream
beneath the feet of joggers,
    clad in sleek apparel
        working nature's runway
            with European confidence
All construction, utilitarian
reflecting soft, constant sunlight,
and everything feels like it's
at water's edge.

# Those Three Seconds

Show me all the things you hide
Since they broke you into bits and pieces

Sing me the melody I heard
Those three seconds
When your guard dropped

That's where I want you to live
Where I want to live

And let me harmonize

Let me harmonize.

Strum me how your heart beat
Before it
Broke

Let me feel your strength
Before it
Waned

Let my pride restore the glory
Muted

Let my hands restore the flinch
Instilled

Let my faithfulness restore the trust
Devoured

Let my heart ignite the spark
Extinguished

Let the possibility
Disarm and unharden

And bring us back to life

This short life.

# Sweet Gibberish

Some of the sweetest words
I've ever heard were:
No-uh-pah-tah
Gobba Gobba No
And
Cavidividee.

# Underneath

Beams radiate underneath
And he holds them close
His Aces are inside
But a counsel of Jokers awaits
To jar the beams
Of which mere glimpses could blind
An almost holy man—
And he lets them

A tripartite battle for dominance
Of bodily organs
A new winner reigns
Each day, each week

But
One day he met a stranger
A cold stranger
And he warmed him
With frankincense and myrrh
And black onyx
And that stranger stayed awhile
But not for long

And
One day he met a stranger
A cold stranger
Who would not be warmed
By all these things
And that stranger could not stay
For long

But
One day he'll know a man
A cold man, A bold man
Who will not be turned away
Who will harness the beams
Underneath
And lead them to freedom
And by them, be warmed

# Bubble

Descending upon Dominica,
    Countless shades of green paint the mountains
    With unmatched tones and textures
Landing at a strip, no more than a small garage barely standing by
    A jeep awaiting to thump me an hour to
    The Fort Young Hotel
A French Syrian guide greets me at sunrise
    For a hike to Boiling Lake

We drive through the outskirts of Roseau
    Where shades of black and brown hands
    Sling boxes at the docks,
    Squeeze fruit at the markets

We pack sandwiches, whole eggs, bananas, and nuts
    (and I secretly question my endurance,
    flatlander that I am)

We stretch and set off up and down the steepest hills
    Scrambling over rocks, water whooshing over
    Wading across rushing rivers
    Negotiating edges of steep cliffs, hugging trees for support

The smell of Sulphur stings the nose as we approach
    The Valley of Desolation where the green mostly vanishes
    And one wrong step will break the crust
    And remove the skin from our feet

Gray mineral mud streams over the surface
        I paint it on my face in tradition and sound
        A mighty Whitman Yawp.

We find a useful stick to anchor our eggs
        And boil them in the ground for nourishment

When we reach our destination,
I BUBBLE with the fumarole
        Knowing that I have earned a rare sight,
        Remembering all the barriers that might have kept me away,
And thankful that I have
        endured.

# To The Victor

I hid a box in Runyon Canyon
Small and brown, to be found
By one whose eyes
Are not dazzled by the stars
Above or below.

I hid it near a rock
To be unlocked
By one whose hands
Shake from overworking
All of last night's hours.

I hid it near a tree
For he
Whose hands are darker
Than the box.

I hid it off the path
At last
For one who dares
To go that way.

And I long to hear
What's in it.
Someday.

# Alloy

Bound. Breaker.
Abandoned. Celebrated.
Weary. Invigorated.
Man at the counter who speaks like a four-year-old.
Scholar whose words sound fit at once for print.

Redeemed. Unrepenting.
Repulsive. Attractive.
Browbeaten beggar. Generous stranger.
Man waiting for the bus with plastic bags
        filled with rolls of paper towels.
Lingerer idling in heated seats.

Red stater. Blue stater.
Server. The served.
Lead. Day player.
Childless old man struggling to fasten his sandals
        around swollen ankles.
Fit bachelor wearing out the treadmill.

Warmonger. Peace protester.
Prude and celibate. Free and fucking.
Blue collar. Bleached collar.
City boy in shined shoes and fitted suits.
Wallflower in leisurely hats and hoodies.

Outspoken. Stammerer.
Raiser of hand. Sinker into chair.
Brave. Deserter.
Discarder of useful things.
Joad who collects them at the curb.

Unmedicated. Addicted.
Frugal. Lavish.
Indifferent. Invested.
Scrawny and pale, sweating underneath
            black clothes in the summer sun.
Shirtless athlete swaggering the sands of Paradise Cove.

Melt it down, all of it.
Take it in, all of it.
Symbiotic, all of it.

All of it, alloy.

# Little Bird

Little bird, broken wing
Scared little bird
Wary of my intentions
I sang to you, little bird
And now you sing
But you don't sing
For me.

           Little bird, small and frail
           Trembling little bird
           Latches onto me
           I fed you, little bird
           And now you feed
           But you don't feed
           From me.

Little Bird, all alone
Trusting little bird
Gives itself to me
I taught you, little bird
And now you learn
But you don't learn
From me.

           Fly away, little bird
           I loved you for a time
           It hurts that you don't
           Need me now
           But you were never mine.

# Vitamin D

Don't cry for me.

I won't settle,
But I take my vitamin D.

The bones are thick.
They come for me.

I fly solo,
But I take my vitamin D.

No osteoporosis.
No deficiency.
No stand-ins.
No seat fillers.

Don't need your empathy.

So, save that head tilt.
Dry those tears.
And make a cup of tea.

And I'll be here
with my supply
of ample vitamin D.

# High

It's always a plane crash
In his dreams
But in the nosedive
He calmly closes his eyes and
Bows his head
Warm with who he is and
Content with what he leaves behind
Before he fades
To wake

# Omega

All is peaceful
when you know the ending.

You let go
when you're sure of it.

And I am sure.

Betas may come and go,
      linger now and then,
            or maybe even stay a while

But my bones, they know.
They pop and crackle Morse code.

      You. are. the. Omega. They say.

The trees, they whisper
The moon, it projects
The smoke, it writes:

Rest easy.

You are the Omega.

# Give Me A Mountain

To calm the devil's yawp
Give me a Mountain

To suffer through the day
Give me a Climb

To clean a muddy spirit
Give me Clouds

To fortify a body
Give me Sky

To still a labored soul
Give me Rivers

To steady wobbly hands
Give me Trees

To clear an anxious mind
Give me Glaciers

To bind me to the ground
Give me Earth.

These are all I need.

*Know that you are loved.*

-A

www.ingramcontent.com/pod-product-compliance
Lightning Source LLC
Chambersburg PA
CBHW020400130626
46549CB00006B/2363